BIG CITY Greens

THIS BOOK BELONGS TO

. . . .

THANK YOU FOR BEING OUR VALUED CUSTOMER. WE WOULD BE GRATEFUL IF YOU SHARED THIS HAPPY EXPERIENCE ON AMAZON.

THIS HELPS US TO CONTINUE PROVIDING GREAT PRODUCTS, AND HELPS POTENTIAL BUYERS TO MAKE CONFIDENT DECISIONS

COLOR TEST PAGE

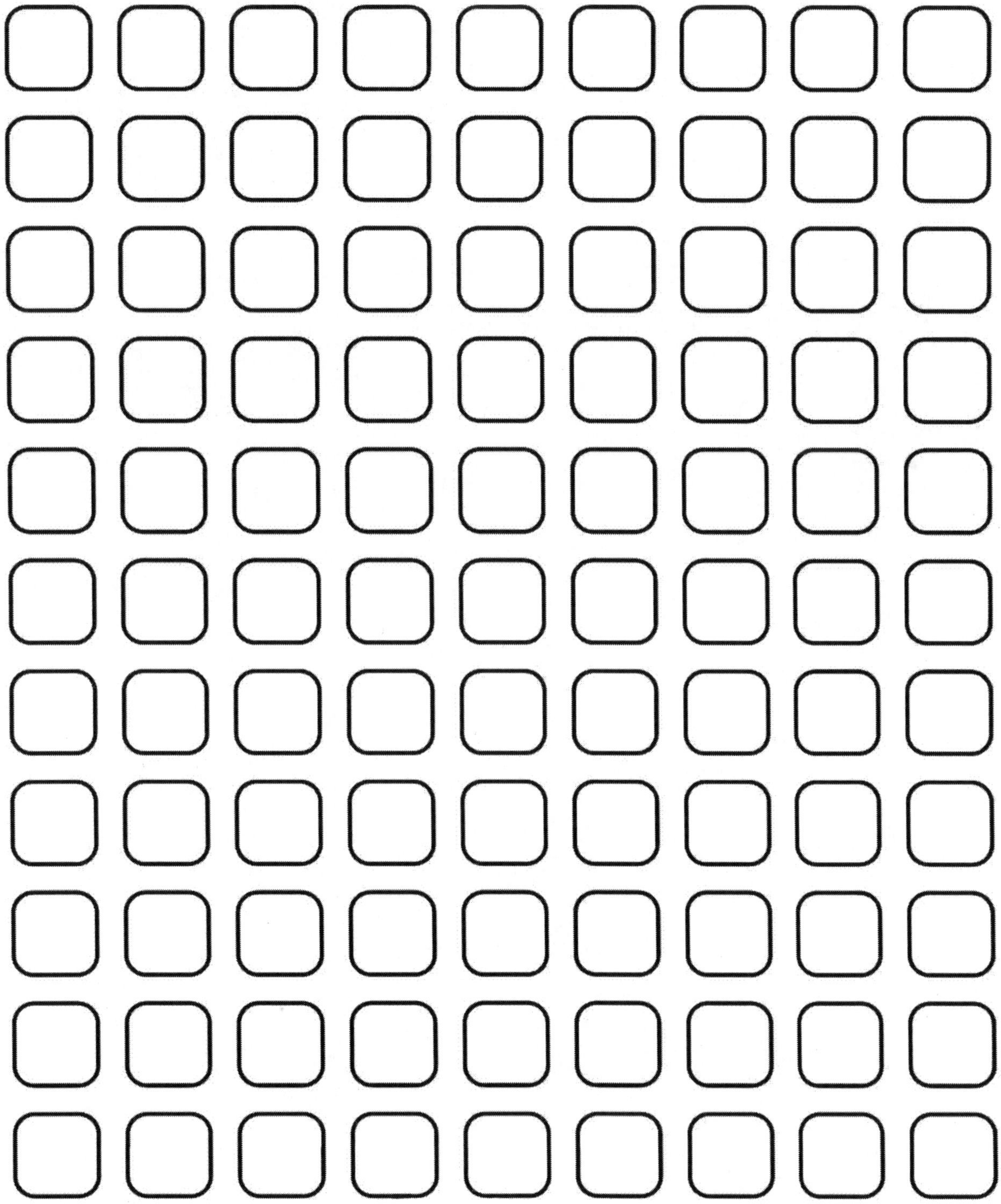

BIG CITY
Greens

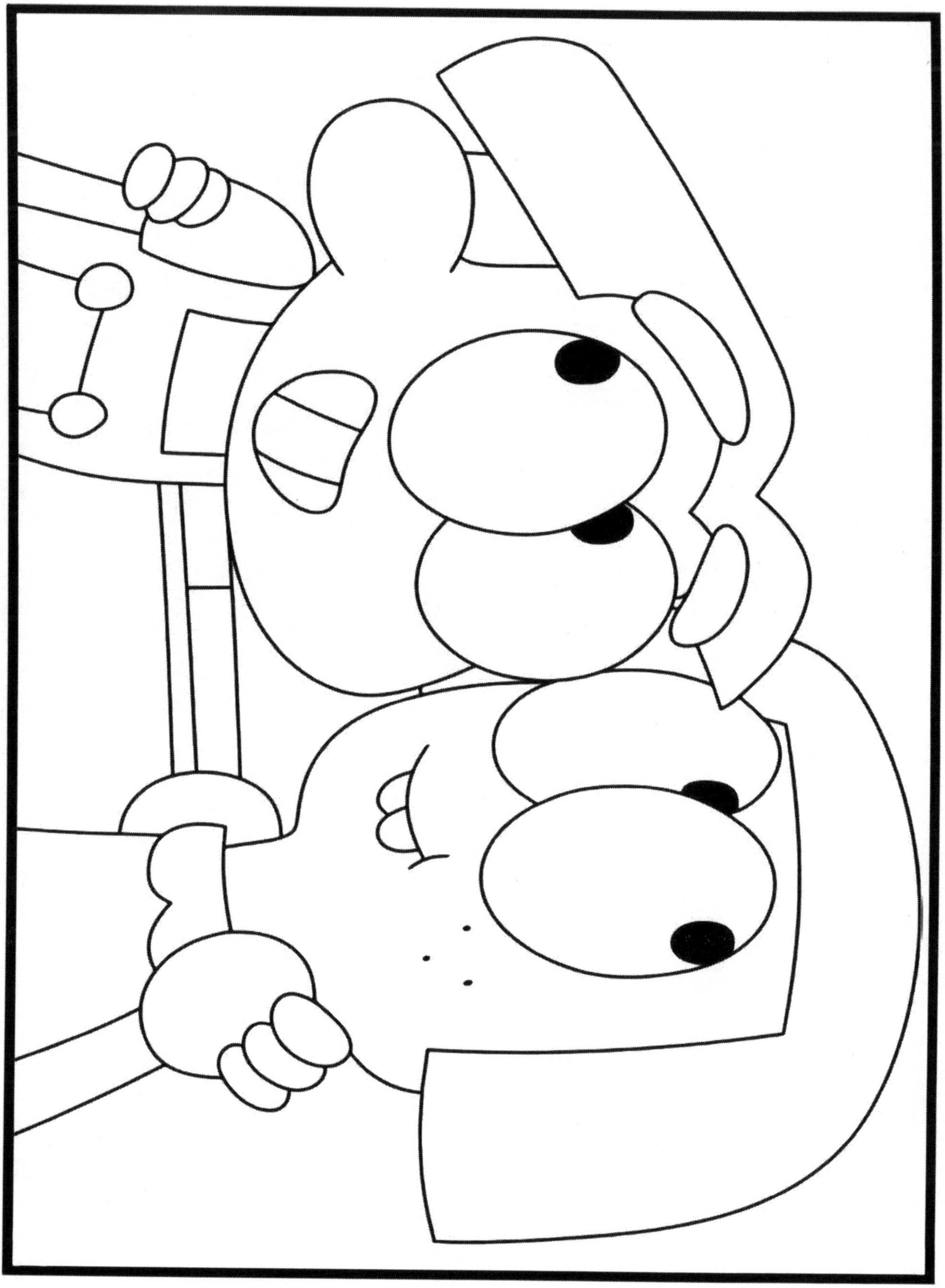

BIG CITY
Greens

Made in the USA
Las Vegas, NV
04 December 2024

13335661R00031